TECH **TITANS**

NETFLIX

BY ALEXIS BURLING

CONTENT CONSULTANT

Myles McNutt
Assistant Professor, Communication and the Arts
Old Dominion University

Essential Library

An Imprint of Abdo Publishing | abdobooks.com

ABDOBOOKS.COM

Published by Abdo Publishing, a division of ABDO, PO Box 398166, Minneapolis, Minnesota 55439. Copyright © 2019 by Abdo Consulting Group, Inc. International copyrights reserved in all countries. No part of this book may be reproduced in any form without written permission from the publisher. Essential Library™ is a trademark and logo of Abdo Publishing.

Printed in the United States of America, North Mankato, Minnesota.
092018
012019

THIS BOOK CONTAINS RECYCLED MATERIALS

Cover Photo: Guillaume Payen/SOPA Images/LightRocket/Getty Images
Interior Photos: Gabby Jones/Bloomberg/Getty Images, 4–5; Red Line Editorial, 6, 60, 80; Suzanne Kreiter/The Boston Globe/Getty Images, 9; Paul Sakuma/AP Images, 14–15, 23, 36–37, 46–47, 53, 65, 72–73; Rick Bowmer/AP Images, 18; Suamy Beydoun/AGIF/AP Images, 24–25; John Todd/AP Images, 26; Shutterstock Images, 31, 89; Justin Sullivan/Getty Images, 35, 44; Stevan Morgain/AP Images, 42; Dale Wilcox/WireImage for Netflix/Getty Images, 49; Vivien Killilea/Getty Images, 50; Donna McWilliam/AP Images, 57; WaveBreakMedia/Shutterstock Images, 58–59; Scott Anderson/Journal Times/AP Images, 67; Netflix Inc./AP Images, 70; FG/Bauer-Griffin/GC Images/Getty Images, 77; Kiyoshi Ota/Bloomberg/Getty Images, 85; Africa Studio/Shutterstock Images, 86–87; Dirk Steinmetz/picture-alliance/dpa/AP Images, 91; Paolo Bona/Shutterstock Images, 94; Rolf Vennenbernd/picture-alliance/dpa/AP Images, 96

Editor: Arnold Ringstad
Series Designer: Laura Polzin

Library of Congress Control Number: 2018948316

Publisher's Cataloging-in-Publication Data

Names: Burling, Alexis, author.
Title: Netflix / by Alexis Burling.
Description: Minneapolis, Minnesota : Abdo Publishing, 2019 | Series: Tech titans | Includes online resources and index.
Identifiers: ISBN 9781532116902 (lib. bdg.) | ISBN 9781532159749 (ebook)
Subjects: LCSH: Netflix (Firm)--Juvenile literature. | Video-on-demand--Juvenile literature. | TV shows--Juvenile literature. | Technology--Juvenile literature.
Classification: DDC 384.55506--dc23

CONTENTS

CHAPTER ONE

NETFLIX'S DEEP POCKETS

Toward the end of 2017, the internet media company Netflix made a headline-grabbing announcement. In 2018, it would spend between $7 billion and $8 billion on original and acquired content. That's a whopping $1 billion more than it spent in 2017 on smash hits such as *Stranger Things* and *13 Reasons Why*.[1] The amount is also equal to or larger than the spending budgets of many other streaming providers or traditional TV media companies for programs other than sports, including HBO, FX, CBS, Hulu, and even tech giant Amazon.

Netflix is not only spending large amounts of money, it is making money as well. In just three months in 2017, the company raked in nearly $3 billion in revenue from domestic and international subscriptions. During those same three months, Netflix's net income rose to

Stranger Things, which debuted in 2016, became one of Netflix's biggest hit shows.

NONSPORTS SPENDING BY TV AND INTERNET STREAMING COMPANIES, 2017[5]

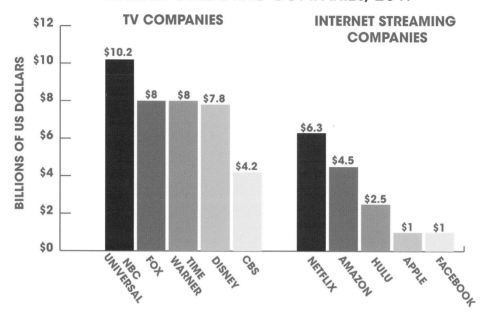

In 2017, many companies in both traditional television and internet streaming spent $1 billion or more on nonsports programming.

$130 million. That's $78 million more than the company made during the same period in 2016.[2]

Since its founding in 1997, Netflix has transformed from a DVD sales and rental company into the largest internet entertainment service provider in the world. After picking up 8.3 million new subscribers in the last three months of 2017, it had more than 117 million paying members in more than 190 countries.[3] These subscribers collectively watch more than 140 million hours of TV shows and movies per day.[4]

How has Netflix become so successful? The company's services, whether it is delivering DVDs by mail or streaming content online, have proven extremely popular with consumers. The company now creates its own original series, award-winning documentaries, foreign films, and programming for kids in order to provide its customers with a steady flow of new things to watch. In addition, Netflix keeps close track of the types of movies and TV shows its customers are watching. The company then uses this data to create and acquire content geared toward the viewing habits of specific audiences. For Netflix and its subscribers alike, it's a win-win situation.

"Netflix is, to the naked eye, a two-pronged success. If your company can produce local content that people love worldwide and you only

NETFLIX WINS ITS FIRST OSCAR FOR A FEATURE FILM

Netflix is no stranger to accolades. The internet media giant has been nominated for, and even won, some major awards before. But from the time it started creating original content in 2013 until 2018, it had never won an Academy Award for a feature-length film.

In March of that year, that changed with the win for Best Documentary Feature. *Icarus* tells the true story of the widespread use of performance-enhancing drugs by Russian professional athletes. It stars Grigory Rodchenkov, the head of Russia's anti-doping agency, who broke the news about the problem. His revelations led to a ban on Russians participating in the 2018 Winter Olympic Games in PyeongChang, South Korea, though some athletes were eventually reinstated.

charge them $8 or €8 a month, you'll land and expand. You'll grow and grow and grow," said Jim Cramer, host of CNBC's *Mad Money.* "The more Netflix knows about what people love, what you love, the more it can scale that love into . . . subscribers."[6]

A MAJOR SUCCESS STORY

In the 2010s, Netflix made some important decisions that paid off and ultimately transformed the company's business model. The first major success story happened as the result of a risky venture. On February 1, 2013, Netflix released *House of Cards*, a remake of a 1990 British political drama. The new adaptation was about fictional US Congressman Frank Underwood, a Democrat from South Carolina's 5th congressional district. But Netflix didn't just release one episode at a time, week by week, as is typical for a prime-time series. Instead, the company put the entire first season of 13 episodes online at once for viewers to watch as they wished.

At first, some consumers were skeptical. Would anyone really watch all the episodes in one sitting? And what about spoilers? How could you prevent your friends from talking about what happened in episode five if you were only on episode two? Some members of the media

Some Netflix customers watch the company's programming while doing other activities, such as knitting.

weren't entirely sold on the idea either. They searched for ways to report on an entire season of television without knowing if all their readers had caught up.

For its part, Netflix wasn't worried. "Our viewing data shows that the majority of streamers would actually prefer to have a whole season of a show available to watch at their own pace," said Ted Sarandos, chief content officer of Netflix, in 2013. "Netflix has pioneered audience choice in programming and has helped free consumers from the limitations of linear television. Our own original series are created for multi-episodic viewing, lining up the content with new norms of viewer control for the first time."[7]

It turns out, as Netflix executives expected, the gamble was worth it. The release of *House of Cards*, the highly successful *Orange Is the New Black*, and cult-favorite *Arrested Development* boosted the popularity of a phenomenon called binge-watching. In the past, people used VHS or DVD box sets or cable TV reruns to watch old or previously released episodes of a TV show in a single sitting. But with Netflix, viewers could watch multiple episodes of a *brand-new* television program in rapid succession.

By December 2013, Netflix had the numbers to prove its experiment was a success. In a survey of nearly 1,500 viewers conducted on behalf of Netflix after the release of *House of Cards*, 61 percent of the group admitted to binge-watching content. The study further reported that

DOES BINGE-WATCHING BREED ANXIETY?

Many people immediately jumped on board the binge-watching bandwagon when *House of Cards* was released in 2013. But the new trend did bring up some worry, especially with members of the media. When media critic Richard Lawson was assigned to review the series, his experience was extreme but not atypical:

"I started on episode six, and seven hours later, there I was, blinking my salty eyes and dying for more," Lawson wrote in his review. "The fear, really, was that I'd be left behind if I didn't finish. That of course everyone else would watch the whole thing by the start of the work week and I wouldn't have anything to contribute."[8]

nearly 73 percent of TV streamers said they had positive feelings towards binge streaming.[9]

"I found that binge watching has really taken off due to a perfect storm of better TV, our current economic climate and the digital explosion of the last few years," said Grant McCracken, a cultural anthropologist who contributed to the study. "But this TV watcher is different, the couch potato has awoken. And now that services like Netflix have given consumers control over their TV viewing, they have declared a new way to watch."[10]

A COMPLICATED HISTORY

By prompting the rise of binge-watching, Netflix changed the way people all

BINGING: THE NEW NORMAL

With the release of *House of Cards*, the itch to binge-watch took the world by storm. But it wasn't just a one-time compulsion; the phenomenon kept going. In June 2016, Netflix introduced The Binge Scale, which placed shows on a sliding scale. The types of shows viewers prefer to savor slowly were on one end of the spectrum, and the types they love to devour all at once were on the other.

First Netflix studied the viewing of more than 100 serialized TV series across more than 190 countries. Then it placed each on the spectrum in terms of the qualities that made the show either habit-forming or something that might inspire calm, delayed viewing. On the slow, thought-provoking end were shows like comedies *BoJack Horseman* and *Unbreakable Kimmy Schmidt*. Those that were most likely to inspire steady viewing were thrillers such as *Breaking Bad*, *Dexter*, and *Sons of Anarchy*.

over the world interact with media content. The move also inspired other media companies to follow suit. Since 2013, other big players, such as Amazon, have produced TV series that can be watched over the course of a few sittings.

But Netflix wasn't always a trendsetting tech titan worth billions of dollars. In fact, when its first website launched in 1998, the company had barely a handful of employees. They worked out of one conference room in a barren office park in California.

Over the course of its more than two decades in business, Netflix has faced a lot of challenges and made some poor decisions. At first, the company sold DVDs in addition to renting them. One of its cofounders left, much to the dismay of some of his staff. In the company's more recent years, some of its original content—including the 2017 film *Bright*, starring Will Smith—was either critically panned or didn't hit the mark with viewers.

Still, despite setbacks, the strength of Netflix as a company continues to rise. In 2017, Netflix's international subscriber pool surpassed the size of its user base in the United States for the first time—more than 62 million compared to nearly 55 million.[11]

In the end, it is the company's willingness to not only celebrate achievements but also learn from shortcomings and make adjustments that has led to its steady growth. "We still have a lot to learn," said cofounder and chief executive officer (CEO) Reed Hastings in 2017. "Now, we've done awfully well in Latin America and in Europe and of course, in North America. So, we've learned some things. But we have a lot of room to grow in Asia and a lot to figure out still."[12]

NETFLIX FLOPS

Stranger Things, *Master of None*, and *Glow* are among the successful programs on Netflix. But the company has also been responsible for producing more than a few shows over the years that were either panned by critics or snubbed by consumers.

The 2017 series *Gypsy*, starring Naomi Watts, is about a psychologist who develops dangerously close relationships with her patients. Though the show had many fans, a critic from the *Village Voice* said, "It's all fun and games until you desperately start hoping that your protagonist loses her malpractice suit."

Marvel's Iron Fist, also released in 2017, was similarly well received by audiences but hated by many critics. "This series takes everything good Marvel has done, takes it on a joy ride, then returns it scratched, bruised, and smelling like patchouli and broken promises," wrote one reporter from *Vox*. "After the 13-hour slog, I'm not angry—I'm just disappointed."[13]

A EUREKA MOMENT

I t was a sunny spring day in Scotts Valley, California, in 1997. A beat-up Volvo station wagon drove into a commuter parking lot and parked next to a shiny Toyota. As the Volvo came to a stop, Reed Hastings, the driver of the Toyota, jumped out of his car. "It came!" Hastings said, with a smile on his face.[1]

At the time, Hastings was in his mid-30s. Just a few weeks earlier, on April 7, he had sold Pure Atria Corporation, the software company he founded in 1991, to a larger firm called Rational Software. The deal was worth approximately $585 million in stock. It was the largest merger in the history of Silicon Valley, Northern California's tech hub.

For months before Pure Atria's sale, Hastings had been meeting 38-year-old Marc Randolph, the driver of the Volvo, in that same commuter

Reed Hastings, Netflix's founder, quickly upended the movie rental industry with his new company.

parking lot. Toward the end of 1996, Hastings had acquired the software start-up where Randolph worked as the chief of product marketing. Instead of firing Randolph, Hastings had hired him to be the head of corporate marketing for Pure Atria. They often carpooled and took turns making the hour-long drive to work.

During the tech boom of the early 1990s, start-up companies were bought and sold with rapid frequency, sometimes for huge sums of money. When a larger company bought a smaller one, some of the start-up's employees were often kept on staff as paid consultants for a few months to help with the transition. Such was the case with Hastings and Randolph at Rational Software.

STRETCHING THE TRUTH

Since the company's founding in 1997, the story of how Netflix really started has evolved. Over the years, facts have been mixed with fiction. The official story, at least in its early days, was that CEO Reed Hastings had misplaced his video rental of *Apollo 13* and had owed $40 in late fees. In a 2006 interview with CBS News, Hastings claimed this unfortunate mishap provided the spark that led to the idea for a subscription video-rental service.

"I was on the way to the gym and I realized—'Whoa! Video stores could operate like a gym, with a flat membership fee.' And it was like 'I wonder why no one's done that before!'" Hastings said.[2]

Cofounder Marc Randolph discredited the story. He claimed this version of events never happened. In later interviews, Hastings admitted "there was no Aha! moment" and that he had stretched the truth.[3]

It was during those early morning commutes to and from Rational Software that the two men started hashing out ideas for a new business venture. Hastings planned to go to graduate school to study education, one of his passions. He agreed to be a mostly off-site partner, at least at first. He also promised to invest $2 million to help get things started.

Randolph wasn't sure what he wanted to do, but he had a hunch that whatever it was would make good use of his past experience in marketing and e-commerce. "These [commutes] were very wide-ranging sessions and they basically started by one of us getting in the car and saying, 'What's the criteria for something that is going to be successful?' Or 'What's a trend that we could leverage?'" he told *Silicon Valley Business Journal*.[4]

One trend everyone in Silicon Valley was familiar with was Amazon founder Jeff Bezos's success with selling books online. By 1997, Amazon had ballooned from a start-up in Bezos's garage to a $12 billion global business. Hastings and Randolph wanted to do something similar. But what would their product be, and how would it fit in with the rest of the technological advances and start-up ventures cropping up in the 1990s?

TECHNOLOGY IN THE 1990s

The 1990s was a volatile decade in the United States, especially concerning matters of technology. The use of personal computers and email was rapidly spreading, but they were significantly less common than they would become in the 2000s. Former US president Bill Clinton, who served from 1993 to 2001, sent a mere two emails the entire time he was in office. People listened to music on their living room stereos and on portable CD players. They shopped for CDs, books, computer games, and anything else they might want in physical stores.

In the 1980s and 1990s, physical stores such as Blockbuster played a central role in the home entertainment industry.

In contrast, listening to music on the internet was clunky, and downloading songs took a long time. Matters improved in 1997, when the MP3 audio format rose in popularity. The format made file sizes smaller. It also made it easier to share music illegally online. Still, streaming music was difficult. Most people in the 1990s used dial-up modems to connect to the internet using their phone line. Slow speeds and sudden interruptions in service were frustratingly common.

THE 1990s VIDEO STORE EXPERIENCE

During the 1990s, people who wanted to rent a movie went to a physical store. All the movies available to rent were stocked in clunky plastic cases on rows of shelves. Most stores usually carried one or two copies of older videocassette tapes. They stocked four or five copies of popular new releases.

When renting a movie, customers had a few days to watch the video before returning it. Tapes had to be rewound back to the beginning before returning them. New releases had to be returned the next day by midnight. Late fees cost a dollar or more per day. The fee for a lost video could cost $60 to $80.

However, the tech landscape was changing rapidly, especially in telecommunications. By the mid-1990s, cell phones had become widely available, giving people more options for communicating with friends and family. Technological advances were affecting the movie industry too. In the early 1990s, the majority of people who watched videos at home rented bulky rectangular VHS tapes to watch on their videocassette recorders (VCRs). The three major video-rental chains were Blockbuster, Hollywood Video, and Movie Gallery.

But in 1997, a new format was released: the digital versatile disc (DVD). DVDs were shaped like compact discs (CDs) but could store much more data. They could play movies and other types of video programming. The invention of the DVD was the biggest leap in video technology yet. It would not only impact the businesses of the big three video chains but also provide the means for Hastings and Randolph to create their new company.

THE DVD REVOLUTION

At first, consumers were hesitant to adopt the new

THE CLASH OF THE VIDEOCASSETTE TITANS

Prior to the advent of DVDs, people watched movies on videocassette tapes. The tapes featured a plastic casing with magnetic tape inside that was wound between two wheels. Inside a VCR, this magnetic tape passed over a set of playback heads that read the data on the tape.

During the 1980s and early 1990s, two video formats dominated the videocassette industry: Betamax and Vertical Helical Scan (VHS). Sony created the first Betamax videocassette in 1975. It could record and play videos that were an hour long. VHS was invented by Japan Victor Company (JVC) in 1977. It was cheaper to buy and could hold up to three hours of content.

For ten years, the two companies had a war over which format would prevail. VHS won out. All production of Betamax tapes in the United States ceased in 1993.

technology. Beginning in 1997, the first DVD players were released in the United States. Most were prohibitively expensive, costing around $1,000 for a basic model.[5] Movie studios initially resisted the DVD format too. They were waiting to see if DVDs took off before they made a serious investment. Earlier formats, such as LaserDisc, had failed to catch on with a wide audience.

But Hastings and Randolph weren't deterred. At the time, there were fewer than 1,000 movie titles available on DVD.[6] Most video stores still sold and rented mostly videocassette tapes. Still, the fact that DVD technology was so new worked to Randolph and Hastings's advantage. They could get in on the ground floor of a potentially new phenomenon. Their idea was to rent DVDs by mail, without the late fees that customers

AN IDEA FOR THE GARBAGE PILE

When Hastings and Randolph were brainstorming ideas for a new business, they came up with a lot that didn't pan out. One early idea was a mail-order VHS tape rental company. It didn't make the cut because shipping the tapes was too expensive. The business model was also financially unfeasible.

"There were [some] fairly geeky problems about what those VHS tapes cost based on the model that studios used . . . . It'd cost you $70, $80 or $100," Randolph said in an interview with *Silicon Valley Business Journal*. "A business like ours, which couldn't turn them 30 times a month like a Blockbuster could, couldn't make it work. So that idea went into the garbage pile."[7]

hated at traditional video-rental stores. There was still one question: Would it actually work?

VICTORY IN THE PARKING LOT

The day before their fateful 1997 parking lot meeting, Hastings and Randolph had gone to a Santa Cruz, California, music store to buy a CD. They had bought a greeting card envelope and placed the CD inside. Finally, they had put a first class stamp on the envelope, addressed it to Hastings's house, dropped it in a mailbox, and waited to see what would happen.

The next morning in the commuter lot, Hastings had the greeting card envelope in his hand. As Randolph got out of the car, Hastings opened the card. Inside was the CD. It had no scratches. It wasn't broken. It was perfect. "That was the moment where the two of us looked at each other and said, 'This idea just might work,'" Randolph told the *Silicon Valley Business Journal*.[8]

The road ahead wasn't going to be easy. In order to be successful, Hastings and Randolph's new business venture would not only have to make enough money to stay afloat, it would also have to take on Blockbuster, Hollywood Video, and Movie Gallery. Even more daunting,

Once Hastings and Randolph discovered mailing discs was feasible, they knew their new company had a chance at success.

the fledgling company would have to convince millions of people to change their well-worn habits in order to embrace a new way of renting movies. A mail-order DVD rental company was incredibly risky. The possibility of failure was high. But Hastings and Randolph were ready to take on the challenge.

CHAPTER THREE

FOUNDING NETFLIX

B y the summer of 1997, Hastings and Randolph had found their footing. Ever since they had settled on the idea of a mail-order DVD business for their new venture, they were eager to get all the logistics of their start-up company ironed out. The first priority was to hire some staff.

With Hastings preoccupied with his graduate studies at Stanford University, the company needed a few on-the-ground people who could take care of daily activities efficiently. One of the first people hired was Christina Kish, a woman who had worked with Randolph at the desktop scanner manufacturer Visioneer. She was savvy with money and could help research the competition. Kish was another member of Pure Atria's staff who had been laid off when

Randolph was excited about steering the new company through its risky, uncertain early days.

REED HASTINGS

Wilmot Reed Hastings Jr. was born on October 8, 1960, in Boston, Massachusetts. His great-grandfather Alfred Lee Loomis was a scientist whose research and experiments led to the development of radar, global positioning systems, and the atomic bomb. After high school, Hastings sold vacuum cleaners door to door for nearly a year. He studied mathematics at Bowdoin College, served in the US Marine Corps, and spent two years teaching math in Swaziland, South Africa.

In 1988, Hastings attended graduate school at Stanford University. There, he got a master's degree in computer science. In 1991, when he was 30, Hastings founded Pure Software, a software company that merged with Atria Software in 1996. This new company, called Pure Atria Corporation, was later bought by Rational Software in 1997. By 1998, Hastings and cofounder Marc Randolph had started NetFlix, a DVD-by-mail company that would soon be worth millions and would lead to the shutdown of movie rental giants Blockbuster and Hollywood Video.

Outside of the tech world, Hastings also has an interest in education. From 2000 to 2004 he was president of the California State Board of Education. He donated $1 million to Beacon Education Network to create new charter schools.[1] As of July 2018, Hasting's net worth was $4 billion.[2]

Within two decades, Hastings turned a small DVD rental business into one of the world's most powerful media companies.

the merger went through with Rational Software, so the timing was ideal.

Hastings and Randolph recruited Eric Meyer, a software engineer and web designer who would be responsible for creating the new company's website. Te Smith was brought on board to handle any marketing and publicity needs. She was also the person who would be in charge of finding consumers and persuading them to purchase the company's products and services. Vita and Boris Droutman, a computer programmer couple in their twenties, would write most of the website's code and fix any errors. Jim Cook became the company's vice president of operations.

Finally, in November 1997, Randolph convinced Mitch Lowe to join the team as video rental expert and chief of movie acquisitions. Randolph had met Lowe at the annual Video Software Dealers Association (VSDA) convention in Las Vegas, Nevada, just a few months prior. At the time, Lowe owned ten retail stores, called Video Droid, across Marin County in Northern California. He also built websites to manage customer databases for video rental stores and was the president of VSDA. Though Lowe was initially skeptical that a video-by-mail business model would work, in the end he was too curious to refuse Randolph's offer.

Now that the core team had been assembled, it was time to prepare for the launch. Over the course of six months, the team met up over burgers and fries at local restaurants. They worked late into the night in order to come up with the nuts and bolts of what was to become their new company.

DRAFTING A BUSINESS PLAN

By the fall of 1997, Randolph and his team had grown tired of taking up space and drinking bad coffee in restaurant booths. So they moved into an old bank in Scotts Valley, California, and converted it to an office space. It had one large main room, a small office for Randolph, a shared office for Kish and Smith, and a conference room. The armored closet, which used to be a vault for money, stored the 500 or so DVD titles they had on hand. Whiteboards were hung on the wall so the staff could map out design concepts.

Once the office was set up, the team started solidifying their first business plan. They came up with dozens of ideas, only some of which stuck. One winning concept, called FlixFinder, was a search engine that customers could use to locate movies by actor, title, or director. Another was FilmFacts, which provided film summaries, ratings, a list of the movie's cast and crew, and a section that described any extra features on the DVD. A feature called Browse the Aisles would allow renters to search through a list of movies in a particular genre, much like they would do if they visited an actual video store.

In between brainstorming sessions, Smith experimented

IDEAS FOR THE FUTURE

Before NetFlix.com launched, Randolph and his team figured out many aspects of the website that were executed right away. But they also kept a list of other projects they wanted to implement in the future. Some of these ideas included a recommendation service that would be able to suggest other movies to watch based on a user's past viewing history, a reminder function that allowed users to keep track of the movies they wanted to watch at a later date, and a subscription plan that would give consumers the option of choosing a certain number of DVDs per month at a fixed price. These features all eventually came to the service.

with more than 200 versions of the size, color, and padding of the packaging that would transport the DVDs from the company's offices to customers' homes. Kish and Meyer mapped out what would soon become the company's first website. Kish wanted the site to be as user friendly as possible, so she used crayons to sketch out how a potential customer should navigate from the home page to the browsing pages and finally to checkout and payment. Meanwhile, the Droutmans, with the help of Cook, created software programs that would allow them to keep track of inventory, take credit card payments, and calculate sales. They set up the program to handle ten million user transactions at the most. Everyone figured they'd be lucky to get 100 orders in the first month.

As months passed, Randolph and his crew began to finalize their business plan. The company would sell and rent DVDs. To rent one DVD, customers would pay four dollars plus two dollars in shipping and handling. Each additional DVD would cost three dollars. Customers could borrow DVDs for up to seven days. If they liked the DVD and wanted to keep it, they had the option to buy it for 30 percent of what it would normally cost in the store.

One key benefit of the new company was that customers would not have to drive to a store to return rented movies.

The last step before the company's launch was to come up with a name. The process was surprisingly difficult. The group agreed that because the business would involve movie rentals and a website, the name should have something to do with film and something to do with the internet. But what? Some suggestions, such as Kibble Inc., were thrown out immediately. Others, including Replay.com, Directpix.com, NowShowing.com, eFlix.com, and CinemaCenter.com, stuck around for a while but were eventually discarded. In the end, the group decided on NetFlix.com. It would be paired with a purple and white company logo that showed a reel of film unspooling.

After more than six months of working, including some nights spent sleeping in the office, Randolph, Kish, and the rest of the NetFlix team were ready. They had made the smart decision to put a bar code on the mailer that would allow it to bypass the high-speed sorting machines at the post office. This would prevent the DVDs from getting crushed. They had done physical drills to see how fast the DVDs could be located on the shelves, packed into mailers, and sorted into mail sacks. They had also recruited consultant Corey Bridges to build buzz with early adopters in the tech community. He frequented popular internet chat rooms to gauge interest in a DVD mail-order rental service. He also contacted early bloggers, who in turn promoted NetFlix and its services to their online communities. With these and other promotional efforts, it was time to put all of the NetFlix team's hard work to the test.

GO TIME

On the morning of April 14, 1998, six months after the first line of code for the website was written, Randolph and his team were finally ready for the NetFlix website to go live. Smith had scheduled a press conference. Reporters from the *San Jose Mercury News*, *Red Herring*, CNET, and other tech-related or investing publications were there to see the event. The members of the NetFlix team were nervous. But they were confident they had done everything they could to prepare.

A LAUNCH-WORTHY CONTEST

To coincide with the company's launch on April 14, NetFlix held an online sweepstakes to attract subscribers. The contest promoted the April 21 DVD release of the Academy Award-winning film *L.A. Confidential*. Anyone who filled out an entry form on the NetFlix website was eligible to win. A purchase wasn't necessary. The winner received a trip to Los Angeles. The whirlwind trip included up to $1,000 for round-trip airfare for two, up to $300 for two nights in a hotel, up to $200 for ground transportation, and up to $500 in cash.[3]

"You get to a certain point in any startup—and you've probably talked to enough of them to know—you just can't research any more. There is just nowhere to look and say, how is the video rental store on CDs, DVDs going to work? The only way to do it is to jump," Randolph later told the *Silicon Valley Business Journal*.[4]

Almost immediately after the website went live, orders flooded in. First ten. Then 20. Suddenly, 90 minutes into the process, the unthinkable happened. The servers reached their capacity and the website crashed. Then the laser printer jammed. Boris Droutman drove at top speeds to a local computer store and back in order to buy ten more computers to boost the website's capacity.

"We have to put up a page on the site saying something like, 'The store is too crowded; come back later!'" Hastings shouted.[5]

Luckily, the website debacle was eventually fixed. Still, more trouble was on the horizon. By that evening, NetFlix had received a large batch of orders. Its staff needed to prepare more than 500 DVDs for shipping before the next morning. If this pace kept up in the weeks and months to come, how would the fledgling company ever keep up?

Developing a system for efficiently processing growing numbers of DVD rental orders would be key to NetFlix's early success.

CHAPTER FOUR

A ROCKY FIRST YEAR

T he year of 1998 was an exciting time for NetFlix and its devoted staff. Impromptu meetings happened at all hours. Decisions were made by consensus. Improvements to established processes took place constantly.

"It had the atmosphere of a laboratory of mad scientists—a creative, unstructured workspace still furnished with worktables. There were no set hours or meetings with agendas—staff members showed up when they needed to be there and stayed as long as it took to finish a project," author Gina Keating writes in her book *Netflixed*.[1]

Still, despite the festive atmosphere, NetFlix's staff struggled to get everything up to speed and running properly in the weeks and months after the company launched. Orders flowed in. But the team had to work overtime to get the DVDs out

The increasing popularity of the DVD format gave NetFlix a constantly growing source of customers in its early years.

on time. The website continued to experience problems as well. Unfortunately, the media noticed.

"We had difficulty using the NetFlix site last week and apparently weren't alone—site carried message 'Sorry, due to extreme opening week demand, the NetFlix Store may be slow,'" a reporter from *Audio Week* wrote. "Spokeswoman said site had 'overwhelming' number of visitors since April 14 launch but couldn't provide specifics on hits."[2]

From the outside, it appeared as though NetFlix had too much to handle. Yet notwithstanding these growing pains, a few factors seemed to be working in NetFlix's favor. In the first six months after DVD players were released on the US market in March 1997, more than 400,000 were sold. By April 1998, the price of a DVD player had dropped from about $1,100 to $580, which meant more consumers could afford to buy one. Movie studios had finally agreed to release their films on DVD. Nearly 100 new titles were made available to consumers every month.[3]

Unintentionally making matters even easier for NetFlix, movie rental giants Blockbuster and Hollywood Video initially decided against stocking DVDs in their stores to maintain their hold on the VHS market. Consequently, customers flocked to NetFlix, which had expanded its list of available DVD titles to 1,500. By the end of the summer, NetFlix had rented out 20,000 DVDs. Its monthly revenue jumped to $100,000.[4] The NetFlix library grew to 2,300 titles.[5]

But in spite of these small successes, NetFlix was still treading water. The staff also had another hiccup to contend with: the return of the company's cofounder, Reed Hastings. He had become disillusioned with graduate school and wanted to take a greater role in managing the company as sole CEO. Not everyone was happy about the adjustment, especially Marc Randolph, who had been effectively running the company by himself for months since the launch. But Hastings was determined to take the company from a little start-up to a growing business that could compete with the biggest and the best in the movie rental industry. His first major move was to slice the company in half and throw one half away.

BIG CHANGES

By the time the November holidays rolled around in 1998, NetFlix needed an influx of cash—fast. Though profits were coming in, the expense of maintaining its operations and a staff that now numbered nearly 100 had also increased.[7] The company would fail if its executives didn't come up with a solution soon.

To cut the company's losses of a projected $11 million, Hastings made a risky decision.[8] At the time, DVD sales provided the company's main source of income. But NetFlix was starting to face major competition from retailers like Walmart and Amazon, which could crush NetFlix's DVD sales and put the company out of business. Something had to give. By December, Hastings decreed that NetFlix would no longer sell DVDs. Instead, it would put all of its focus on rentals.

FAILED PARTNERSHIPS

Ever since his success in founding Pure Software and selling Pure Atria, Hastings had believed in knowing when to cut his losses in order to sell a start-up for a profit. But in NetFlix's first year in business, those attempts to do so didn't work. Hastings approached Bezos in the hope that Amazon would buy NetFlix outright. But he backed out of the deal when Bezos offered only $12 million. Randolph talked to Hollywood Video founder Mark Wattles about buying NetFlix as well. Again, the offer was too low. Instead, Hollywood Video bought Reel.com, one of NetFlix's main rivals. Finally, Hastings met with executives at Blockbuster. They weren't interested either, saying that VCRs were still extremely popular.

"We decided that not only were DVD sales overwhelming the business, but ironically it was making it increasingly less likely that we could be successful with rental, because we were so distracted," Randolph later told the *Silicon Valley Business Journal.* "We can either keep on muddling along and have a reasonable success or we can bet everything on the long shot. But if we hit it, we'll be in a much, much better position."[9]

After a meeting in Seattle, Washington, with Amazon CEO Jeff Bezos, NetFlix agreed to direct any customers who wanted to purchase DVDs to Amazon. In return, Amazon would post ads for NetFlix rentals on its website. Hastings partnered with electronics stores to include coupons for NetFlix rentals for every DVD player sold. In January 1999, Hastings made an additional deal with AllMovie, an extensive database of movies that included reviews, ratings, and biographies of each film's cast and crew. Anyone hoping to find a movie to watch on the site would also see information on how to rent the title on NetFlix. It was a long shot, but Hastings was confident that this improved rental-only business model would make a difference.

NetFlix struck several partnerships, including one with Amazon's Jeff Bezos, in an attempt to establish itself in the marketplace.

TRENDSETTING SERVICES

Now that the DVD sales portion of the company had been cut loose, NetFlix's staff was freed up to make changes to other aspects of the business. They knew their customers loved the convenience of renting DVDs through the mail. But the novelty had worn off. Something needed to be done that would not only entice new customers but also keep the audience NetFlix already had.

By mid-1999, NetFlix's library had expanded to more than 250,000 total discs of new releases and older titles.[10] That September, the company announced a new subscription service, something no other movie rental company was doing at the time. Called the Marquee Plan, the service allowed members to pay $15.95 per month to select four DVDs, with no late fees. Less than five months later, the fee would be adjusted to $19.95 per month for unlimited rentals, with up to three movies checked out at a time.[11] Alongside their subscription, customers could place titles they were interested in watching in a list called their queue. This would allow for automatic mailings of new DVDs once rented DVDs were returned.

"Movie renters are fed up with due dates and late fees," Hastings said in the press release promoting the new program. "NetFlix.com's Marquee program puts the joy back into movie rental. With no due dates, our customers

MISMATCHED PROFITS

In its first few years in business, NetFlix raked in cash. But it also spent a fortune on computers, office space, advertising and marketing efforts to attract new customers, and salaries for its growing staff. As is the case with many technology start-ups, the company was outspending what it was bringing in. In 1999, NetFlix reported losses of $29.8 million on revenues of only $5 million. Two years later, the figures were still mismatched. In 2001, NetFlix brought in $75.9 million. But it still reported losses of $38.6 million for the year.[12]

Hastings was closely involved in the company's operations as it grew in the early years.

can stock up on rental movies and always keep a few on top of their television, ready for impulse viewing."[13] From the moment it launched, the new program was popular with customers.

To build upon the Marquee program's success, NetFlix made another adjustment to its website's offerings in February 2000. It introduced a new service called CineMatch, an algorithm that compared customers' profiles and rental patterns in order to discover similarities in movie-watching habits. The program would then use this information to provide DVD recommendations to people with similar tastes. This personalized movie-rental experience was another big hit with consumers. By April, NetFlix's subscriber base had jumped to 120,000. More than 800,000 DVDs were shipped out per month.[14]

But NetFlix wasn't only paying attention to its customer base. It was expanding and solidifying its relationships with movie studios such as Warner Home Video, Dreamworks, and Columbia Tri-Star too. In exchange for sharing some of the profits from rental receipts, the studios agreed to give NetFlix exclusive content and better prices on large quantities of DVDs. For example, NetFlix subscribers could choose from nearly 1,000 Indian films to rent at any given moment. That's far more than what was available at any brick-and-mortar movie rental location.

After nearly three years in business, NetFlix had yet to break even, just like many tech start-ups. But the company had certainly come a long way from the days of its cofounders' restaurant discussions and late-night hotel brainstorming sessions. For the most part, customers were happy with NetFlix's services. But in the coming months, some big shake-ups were about to take place that would rattle the company to its core. The changes—both positive and negative—would change the way NetFlix functioned in the years to come.

CHAPTER FIVE

NETFLIX RESTRUCTURES

By the end of 2001, the dot-com bubble in the United States had burst. Beginning in March 2000 and stretching out for the next two years, the once-booming tech sector had crashed. Stocks tanked. Companies were losing between $10 and $30 million a quarter. Investors were hesitant to shell out large amounts of money to even slightly unstable tech companies. Some, like Pets.com, folded. Amazon had not yet broken even. Facebook hadn't even been invented. Its founder, Mark Zuckerberg, was still attending high school.

NetFlix was also in turmoil at that time. Though subscription numbers had reached 500,000, the company was still making significant sacrifices.[1] It ended 2001 with a net loss of $38.6 million on revenue of $75.9 million.[2] Consequently, NetFlix had to cut

Netflix went through significant changes in its first few years, including a move to a new headquarters.

nearly 40 percent of its staff. Since Hastings had taken over as sole CEO, many members of the original team had either quit because of the grueling pace or were let go for underperforming, including Vita Droutman and Corey Bridges.

Cook, NetFlix's former vice president of operations, left willingly when he was passed over for a promotion to chief financial officer (CFO). In Cook's place, Hastings hired 45-year-old former investment banker W. Barry McCarthy Jr. to be the company's CFO. He was offered a $170,000 salary with the promise of a $20,000 bonus if he brought in more business. Te Smith also quit and was replaced by 33-year-old Leslie Kilgore, a former marketing executive for Procter & Gamble and Amazon. Christina Kish, who had battled ongoing ailments and a series of stress-induced illnesses, took an extended leave of absence and never returned to work full time. The head of human resources was also laid off.

But the person who arguably suffered the most was the man responsible for coming up with the idea for NetFlix in the first place: Marc Randolph. Though he was designated co-CEO when the company launched in 1998, Randolph was demoted to president a few months later.

Kilgore went on to spend more than a decade at Netflix.

By 2002, he had left the company, though he remained on the board of directors. Finally, he resigned from the board in 2004. All the while, Hastings had moved up from cofounder and chairman to CEO, becoming the sole public face of NetFlix.

Many members of NetFlix's staff were sad to see Randolph's authority stripped and his responsibilities diminished. Unlike Hastings, who was more driven by deadlines and results, Randolph had fostered a festive,

MARC RANDOLPH

Marc Bernays Randolph was born on April 29, 1958, in Chappaqua, New York. Randolph attended Hamilton College in New York. After graduating with a degree in geology, he got a job at Cherry Lane Music Company mailing out music scores to customers. He also designed the company's mail-order catalog and educated himself about direct marketing, a skill he would later use at Netflix.

Following Cherry Lane, Randolph cofounded a series of successful start-ups. In 1984, he helped create the US version of *MacUser* magazine, a publication for users of Apple Macintosh computers. In 1985, he helped start MacWarehouse and MicroWarehouse, two computer mail-order businesses. He designed their mail-order catalogs and helped launch the companies' sales and telemarketing arms. Other tech start-ups he cofounded prior to Netflix include IntegrityQA and Visioneer.

Randolph spent seven years at Netflix in various capacities. In 2012, he cofounded yet another tech start-up, the analytics software company Looker Data Sciences. In 2018, Randolph was a trustee of the nonprofit National Outdoor Leadership School and the environmental advocacy group One Percent for the Planet.

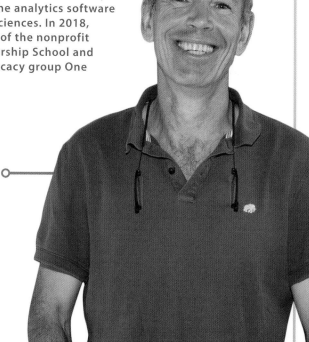

Randolph's experience in marketing and technology helped Netflix get off to a strong start.

creative, family-like atmosphere during his tenure at the company. But despite some speculation that he was forcibly pushed out by Hastings, when it was time for him to leave the company he helped found, Randolph didn't hold a grudge.

"I had enough mileage to begin to recognize there are some things I'm good at, and some things I'm really good at, and some things I'm not very good at. And I believe I am really great at starting companies. I'm pretty mediocre at running them when they begin to hit some scale," Randolph later told *Silicon Valley Business Journal*. "I'm extremely happy, extremely proud of how it worked out. And extremely fortunate I got to work so closely with [Hastings], who I think is the best entrepreneur, not just in the Valley, in the world."[3]

REBRAND AND EXPAND

Now that Hastings had gained full control of NetFlix, he and his handpicked team made major changes to the company's image. As always, it was important to stay current and out in front of the competition, attract new subscribers, and regain the trust of investors with deep pockets.

A VISIONARY MIND

Many historians say that the reason some people succeed over others is that they have vision. They aren't afraid to take risks or fail. But more importantly, they think ahead and plan ways to disrupt the status quo in order to influence the future in positive ways. From the beginning, Hastings had vision. He set goals for the company, and when those goals were accomplished, he set new ones.

"The dream 20 years from now is to have a global entertainment distribution company that provides a unique channel for film producers and studios," Hastings told a reporter from *Wired* in 2002. "Starbucks is a great example. [Starbucks CEO] Howard Schultz talks about building the brand one cup at a time. I'd love to be Howard Schultz. As Starbucks is for coffee, Netflix is for movies."[4]

Since her hiring in 2000, Kilgore had been working on designs for updating the company's branding to make it flashier and more recognizable. She had staged dozens of focus groups to gauge which logo appealed to the most people. She experimented with the size and shape of the lettering, as well as the color of the background. With Hasting's approval, the changes were implemented. The company name was now written in white lettering with a shadowed, three-dimensional effect to make it pop. NetFlix was changed to Netflix, with a lowercase *f*. Finally, the company name was set against a red background to symbolize old-fashioned movie curtains.

In late 2001, the company had also relocated from Scotts Valley to the heart of Silicon Valley, in Los Gatos,

Netflix's new branding would become an iconic part of the company's image as it expanded in popularity.

California. Netflix's new headquarters weren't fancy. Clusters of cubicles were scattered around a big open room. The ceilings were low and the carpet looked dingy. To spruce up the place, Hastings hung movie posters on the walls and installed an old-fashioned popcorn maker in the lobby.

Next, it was time to expand Netflix's distribution capabilities to help facilitate quicker deliveries to customers across the United States. In early 2002, new regional facilities were opened in Los Angeles, California, and Boston, Massachusetts. By early summer, warehouses had opened in Atlanta, Georgia; Denver, Colorado; Detroit, Michigan; Houston, Texas; Minneapolis, Minnesota; New York; Seattle, Washington; and Washington, DC.

Each distribution center was equipped with high-end computers, bar-code scanners, and printers. Nearly 50,000 orders were processed per day. Each order was shipped overnight whenever possible.

By mid-2003, Netflix had more than one million subscribers.[5] The company had also signed deals with

NETFLIX GOES BRICK-AND-MORTAR

Netflix has always been a DVD-by-mail company. But it did experiment with opening one physical location. The store was a large booth in a section of Smith's Food and Drug in Summerlin, a suburb of Las Vegas. It stocked 2,000 DVDs and staffed one employee at all times. The store was originally the brainchild of Marc Randolph and Mitch Lowe and was called Netflix Express.

Customers appeared to love the concept. In fact, the booth reported more activity than expected. But when Lowe told Hastings about Netflix Express's success, Hastings shut down the idea. He claimed inventory costs were too high to be sustainable. The money needed to be invested in digital distribution instead. The store closed less than a month after it opened in 2002.

more than 50 film distributors. The film companies received nearly 20 percent of Netflix's subscription fees in exchange for giving Netflix access to a wide range of movie titles. Netflix's library ballooned to 15,000 DVDs.[6] But the company still wasn't in the clear. It faced mounting competition from other video rental companies that wanted to find their own place in the industry.

COMPETITION HEATS UP

In 2003, two companies posed an immediate threat to Netflix's business model: Walmart and Blockbuster. Walmart.com had just rolled out a new subscription program that looked suspiciously similar to Netflix's plan. The Walmart plan advertised access to 12,000 titles and convenient delivery by mail. Users could check out three movies at a time and wouldn't be subjected to late fees. And while Netflix's plan cost $19.95 a month, Walmart's plan was $18.86.[7]

Blockbuster boasted an even bigger competitive edge. In 2003, it had approximately 9,000 stores worldwide with 20 million in-store customers. Those customers had access to a new subscription plan that would allow them to check out an unlimited number of DVDs in the store for a monthly fee. In addition, executives at Blockbuster were working on an online store that they hoped would lure customers away from Netflix.

Luckily for Netflix, there were inherent problems in Blockbuster's new business model. First, the planned online platform looked almost identical to Netflix's website, which made the company seem like an unoriginal copycat. Second, Blockbuster's online arm was built to be separate from the brick-and-mortar stores so as not to detract from the physical stores' business. Though this program eventually evolved to include a subscription that gave customers access to both the stores and the online offerings, the lack of data sharing between the two segments of the company hurt its success.

Because of these issues, Hastings wasn't worried about Blockbuster overpowering Netflix. "In terms of their online efforts, we expect Blockbuster.com to be approximately as successful against us as Barnes & Noble was against Amazon," he said in a meeting with investors in early 2004. "Until we are sure, however, we plan to watch them closely."[8]

By 2004, Netflix's subscriber numbers were rising rapidly. The company had just launched its first advertisements on television to recruit new customers,

Blockbuster created its own rental-by-mail service, but it was unable to overcome Netflix's lead in this area.

which proved to be successful. In April, Hastings felt confident that business was going well enough to raise the subscription cost to $21.99 a month for three DVDs out at a time. In the years to come, the company would continue to make these types of incremental changes to the Netflix experience. Some of these moves would not only effectively destroy their competition, but they would also transform the company into the most popular movie rental company in the world.

CHAPTER **SIX**

FROM DVDS TO STREAMING

I n the mid-2000s, the world was changing at a rapid pace. Advances in technology were slowly but surely changing not only the way people accomplished tasks but also how they planned out and lived their lives. Slim laptops made it possible for more people to work and enjoy media outside the home. Video game consoles brought about more realistic graphics and new motion-based control methods. Large, flat-panel televisions became more affordable and gained new multimedia capabilities.

One of the greatest breakthroughs was the smartphone. Though cell phones and even touch screens had been around for a while, the world of electronics changed with the release of the first Apple iPhone on June 29, 2007. More than just a phone, the device allowed users to enlarge or shrink photos with their fingers, browse the

The rise of smart devices and broadband internet service boosted the popularity of widespread video streaming.

PERCENTAGE OF US ADULTS WITH BROADBAND INTERNET ACCESS[1]

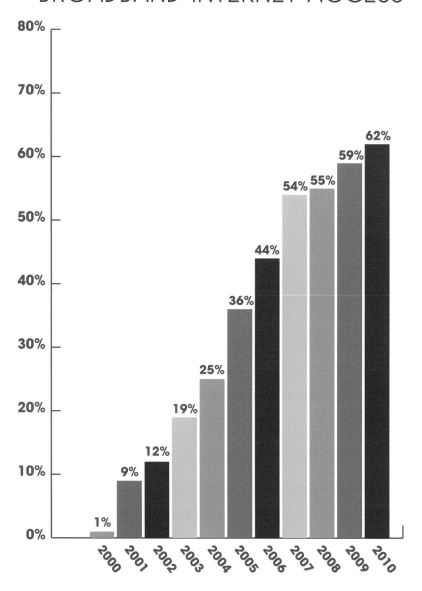

In the decade after 2000, broadband internet access in the United States expanded at a rapid pace. This created a vast new market for online video-streaming services, including the one established by Netflix.

internet, and listen to music. It also made it possible to stream video on the go.

Perhaps the biggest tech-related shift in the mid-2000s was the rise of social media. In 2004, Mark Zuckerberg launched what would eventually become the world's most popular social network, Facebook. At first only accessible to students at American colleges and universities, Facebook later became available to anyone over 13 who had an email address. Facebook users could post photos, connect with friends, and reach out to their friends' friends. The company's success led to the popularity of other social media platforms and to Americans' newfound obsession with maintaining their online image and discussing music, movies, and other forms of culture with their online communities.

Throughout all of these developments, the people at Netflix were keeping a close watch and making adjustments to the company's services. Toward the end of 2005, Netflix introduced a few key changes to its website, hoping to attract new customers. A "Profiles" setting enabled people in families to create separate queues for the same joint account. Jumping on the social media bandwagon, Netflix added a "Friends" option,

THE ROLLING ROADSHOW

Hastings was confident about Netflix's appeal to customers. But partly in response to ongoing pressure from its competition, the company was always looking for fun ways to attract new subscribers. In 2006, Netflix staged a monthlong event it called the Rolling Roadshow. It sponsored a series of screenings of iconic movies at outdoor venues across the United States. Each screening also featured a concert thrown by one of the movie's leading stars or fun-filled activities related to the movie's theme.

In August, an event in Dyersville, Iowa, showed the 1989 film *Field of Dreams*. Kevin Costner, the film's star, also performed with his band. The night was a huge hit. More than 7,000 people attended. "The Netflix Rolling Roadshow underscores Netflix's commitment to making movie enjoyment easy and accessible," said Kilgore. "We hope that members and non-members alike will find the tour an appealing blend of the many film genres and vast library of titles we offer."[2]

which allowed subscribers to share with their online social networks the list of films they wanted to see, along with their movie reviews.

Contrary to Netflix's hopes, neither feature was a big hit. But the company was facing a larger obstacle. Though Walmart had dropped out of the online DVD rental business in 2005 because it couldn't keep up with the competition, Netflix's war with Blockbuster over subscription pricing was heating up. Netflix was scrambling to find ways to come out on top and retain its customers. There was also a new phenomenon to contend with: videos on demand.

A NEW WAY TO WATCH MOVIES

At the end of 2005, Netflix reached a milestone. It had finished out the year with 4.2 million subscribers and no debt. The company's value had reached approximately $1.5 billion.[3]

By 2006, renting and selling of DVDs had become a $27 billion industry.[4] But things were slowly beginning to change. In 2006, about 50 percent of Americans had access to broadband internet service. They experienced faster speeds and less likelihood of a dropped connection. In response, companies created new programs to enable consumers to watch streaming content over the internet.

A CONTEST WORTH $1 MILLION

In 2006, Netflix's CineMatch algorithm was as strong as ever and now applied to viewers' streaming preferences as well. The more movies a subscriber rated, the closer Netflix's movie recommendations would be to his or her tastes. Because of CineMatch, every time a user logged in, he or she would see a unique website tailored to his or her current viewing habits.

But Hastings wanted CineMatch to be even more accurate. So on October 2, 2006, Netflix announced a contest to see who could come up with a new algorithm that would improve CineMatch's prediction rate by 10 percent. Participants could live anywhere in the world, be any age, and have any amount of education. The contest would last three years. Each year, the closest teams would receive $50,000. At the contest's conclusion, the winner would receive $1 million.[5]

More than 40,000 teams in 186 countries entered. Robert Bell and Chris Volinsky, statisticians from AT&T Laboratories, won. They donated their prize to charity.

The ABC network launched the ABC Media Player, which allowed consumers to stream ABC programming for free as long as they agreed to watch TV advertisements between show segments. A group of five major movie studios—Metro-Goldwyn-Mayer, Universal, Warner Brothers, Paramount, and Sony—created Movielink, a web-based video-on-demand service that offered movies, TV programs, and other content for rental or purchase. Though 1,400 titles were available to rent and 1,000 were available for purchase, the project failed after a year because the videos took so long to download.[6]

After much discussion among its staff, Netflix decided against entering the videos-for-download fray. Instead, the company took a different approach. In January 2007, it launched its online streaming service, called Watch Now. There were 1,000 titles available. At first, customers were not charged any additional fees on top of their existing DVD subscription plans. Based on the existing play they had, customers had access to a certain number of streaming hours per month. Hastings hoped the move would not only meet a new and growing market demand but also reduce company costs by chipping away at its reliance upon physical DVDs, stocked warehouses, and postage.

Netflix's streaming service, launched as a side benefit for existing disc-rental customers, would eventually become the central feature of the company's offerings.

Critics praised the new service. "In its ideal form, it is an impressive product: Using a small, easily downloaded application that resides in a user's browser, Netflix detects the user's bandwidth and streams a movie at optimal resolution to avoid pauses to reload. At a basic DSL or cable modem speed, resolution is excellent, and the viewer can pause the movie or download a different film," wrote a reporter from *Forbes*.[7]

By 2008, Netflix had 75,000 titles in its DVD library. After the company partnered with companies such as Roku, LG Electronics, and Microsoft, its content could be accessed by even more consumers on even more platforms. Subscribers could watch Netflix content on laptops, TVs, Blu-ray players, set-top boxes, and mobile devices, as long as they had a membership and access to Netflix software. Through ongoing deals with movie studios, the number of titles available for streaming soon grew to 12,000. In late 2008, the freedom to watch anywhere at any time attracted a whopping 10,000 new-customer sign-ups per day.[8]

Americans loved the freedom of being able to watch content online without having to rent and return DVDs. Many eventually got rid of their DVD players. As internet service speeds improved in 2009 and into the 2010s, some people even dropped their cable subscription altogether in favor of relying on online streaming.

Blockbuster stores across the country closed as the market for physical video-rental stores collapsed.

A PUBLIC RELATIONS NIGHTMARE

Netflix had 60 DVD distribution centers across the country by the spring of 2009. Its subscription base had expanded to ten million people. Though Blockbuster had seen a surge of new subscribers over the last five years, the company was $1 billion in debt and had to close large numbers of stores.[9] In 2010, the company filed for bankruptcy.

In contrast, Netflix was operating with a huge profit. In 2010, Reed Hastings landed on the cover of *Fortune* and was named the magazine's Business Person of the Year. Netflix also expanded into the global market by making its streaming service available in Canada. The move went better than Netflix executives hoped.

"After a short period in Canada we're now talking about other regions in the world, so that's a good indicator," Netflix spokesman Steve Swasey said in an interview with the Canadian Broadcasting Corporation. "We're extremely pleased with the reception in Canada and . . . based on the early success of Netflix.ca we're going to continue our international expansion next year and we're going to allocate significant dollars to it."[10]

But not everything was running totally smoothly for Netflix at the turn of a new decade. At the time, the

NETFLIX GOES GLOBAL

From 2000 to 2009, through fits and starts, Netflix took the United States by storm. In 2010, it was time to take the operation overseas. Beginning in 2010 with Canada, Netflix expanded its business to other countries. In 2011, Netflix's services were made available to people who lived in Latin America and the Caribbean. By 2012, Netflix was available in the United Kingdom, Denmark, Finland, Norway, and Sweden. This international expansion bumped the number of streaming subscribers to 27 million.[11]

number of staff had reached 600.[12] Some employees were not on board with the way Hastings ran the company. They were exhausted after years of round-the-clock work. Barry McCarthy, the company's longtime CFO, left and took $40 million of his Netflix holdings.[13]

Then, in September 2011, Hastings made a decision that would prove to be a terrible blunder. Though many members of his staff were against it, he announced a change to Netflix policies by posting a video on the company's blog on a Sunday night. The video stated that Netflix would separate its DVD-by-mail and streaming businesses into two separate companies. Netflix would be the streaming service, while a new entity called Qwikster would handle DVD rentals. Qwikster subscribers would have to log on to a separate website, set up a separate account with a separate queue, and pay using a separate billing account.

Members of the press criticized the move. Articles ran in the *Atlantic*, the *New York Times*, and other newspapers and magazines nationwide. The public was annoyed, too. One particularly perturbed customer posted a comment on the Netflix site. He wrote: "Terrible idea. Bad after bad

Qwikster was universally criticized, and Netflix scrapped the new business before it even officially launched.

decision. What's next, only offering movies made in the eighties? I'm getting tired of this."[14]

The experiment was a total flop. The Qwikster launch was canceled. Consequently, 100 Netflix staffers lost their jobs.[15] But though the Qwikster debacle hurt business, the damage wasn't permanent. By 2012, Netflix became more valuable than Comcast, the largest cable company in the United States. It had become the world's largest internet movie subscription service, worth $5 billion. The Netflix DVD library contained 200,000 titles—the largest collection in the world. Its streaming service gave customers access to nearly 45,000 movies that could be watched on 700 devices and counting.[16]

Over the next six years, Netflix would continue to attract more customers. It would also do something its cofounders never imagined would be possible when they founded the company in the late 1990s. In 2013, Netflix became its own production studio.

CHAPTER SEVEN

NETFLIX CULTURE

When Netflix was founded in 1998, no one thought a tiny start-up would have the power to disrupt the enormous movie rental industry. But over the course of 15 years, Randolph and Hasting's company had done just that. So what is it like to work at such a trendsetting business? What is it about Netflix's corporate values, beliefs, and hiring and firing practices that sets the company apart, or is Netflix's culture even any different from that of other tech giants?

Throughout the 1990s and 2000s, many tech start-ups were considered desirable places to work because of their long list of employee perks and their laid-back work environments. Gone were the days of stern-looking workspaces stocked with rows of identical cubicles and poor lighting. Instead, some of the most ingenious and forward-thinking tech companies, such as

Two Netflix executives walk through the company's headquarters in 2012.

WORK OR PLAY?

Before the mid-1990s, most office spaces looked similar. They had private offices for executives, cubicles for lower-level workers, and maybe a small kitchen. The décor was stark, usually done in grays or muted colors. Couches were few and far between.

But the tech start-up boom changed everything. Employers started creating work environments they hoped would not only attract the brightest and most capable workers but also inspire them to stay at work instead of going home. Cloud computing company Box installed a giant yellow slide. Google's San Francisco offices have a putting green for playing golf. At game developer Zynga are red vinyl restaurant booths, arcade games, and even foosball tables.

Google, Square, and Skype, resembled college dorm hangout spaces.

"And why not? Silicon Valley has more money than it knows what to do with, and tech contains one of the most competitive labor markets in the country. If a hot-shot engineer can be wooed by the promise of a roof deck and an espresso bar, these renovations will pay for themselves and then some," wrote a reporter from *New York* magazine.[1]

But unlike other companies, Netflix wasn't known for high-end cafeterias with free food, slushy machines, and waffle-making stations. There were no swimming pools or workspace pods to relax in while listening to music. In fact, for a majority of Netflix's early years in business, its offices had developed a reputation for being austere and somewhat depressing.

Once the company became successful, however, its office atmosphere began to change. In 2013, the company initiated an expansion of its old headquarters in Los Gatos to a bigger and brighter campus down the street. The work took a few years to complete. But the improved office space, where Netflix was still located in 2018, was spread across seven buildings and provided a more comfortable working environment than its predecessor.

The older buildings were more traditional and looked similar to regular offices. There were cubicles and glass conference rooms, kitchens on every floor, an open space with desks for the design team, and movie posters on the walls. One of the wackiest perks was the vending machine filled with gadgets and computer

WELCOME TO HOLLYWOOD!

In February 2017, Netflix's 800 Los Angeles–based employees moved into a shiny 14-story office tower on Sunset Boulevard in Hollywood, California. The building rises 200 feet (61 m) off the ground and features a penthouse with a multi-floored balcony.

"A building like this is a statement—of who you are, what you believe, and what you want to do," said Netflix's chief content officer, Ted Sarandos. "It's aspirational for sure, but beautifully functional. That's why we fell in love with this project as soon as we toured it."[2]

Netflix also has satellite offices throughout the area. Among other buildings, the company occupies the Sunset Boulevard mansion where the movie studio Warner Brothers used to be based, and it leases 99,000 square feet (9,200 sq m) of soundstages.[3]

equipment. Prices were listed on the items, but employees didn't have to pay.

Netflix's newer buildings are much fancier and full of glass windows and sleek furniture. One boasts a massive TV in the lobby that streams Netflix content. Nearby is a cabinet full of Emmy Awards the company has won. Another building features padded circular areas with fluffy pillows, where impromptu brainstorming sessions happen frequently. Movie-themed meeting rooms are common, as are outdoor areas where employees can kick back and relax in the sun. There's a large theater where new TV series are played and company gatherings are held. Free beverages and snacks are available, and bikes and electric cars are parked in front in case employees need to travel between buildings in a hurry.

Netflix's offices are not quite as lavish or sophisticated as those at tech companies like Google, Uber, or Skype. But for Hastings and the rest of the executive team, the main objective was to provide a comfortable space in which employees can be ultra efficient and produce optimal results with the least amount of unnecessary distractions. A corporate memo explains, "Our version of the great workplace is not comprised of sushi lunches,

Some of Netflix's newer buildings feature stylish, modern architecture.

great gyms, big offices, or frequent parties. Our version of the great workplace is a dream team in pursuit of ambitious common goals, for which we spend heavily."[4]

GENEROUS REWARDS

Beyond the external upgrades Netflix made to its offices over the years, company executives also focused on making sure their internal culture was the best it could be. One of the ways they did this was to provide their employees with certain perks. A chief reason people choose to work at Netflix is the generous salary that comes with the job. Similar to other tech jobs, the estimated median annual salary at Netflix is high—$134,492, or $64 per hour.[5] That's compared to the highest median mid-career salary in the tech industry, $141,000, at Google.[6] The national median salary is $45,396 per year.[7]

In addition to the impressive salary and the possibility of a year-end bonus for excellent performance, Netflix's full-time employees are also entitled to a generous benefit package. The company's comprehensive vision, dental, and health insurance coverage is considered standard for the industry. But Netflix's life insurance policy is reportedly one of the best in the country.

Most salaried Netflix employees have unlimited vacation, too. Technically, they can go away when they

NETFLIX SALARIES

The salary range for Netflix employees has evolved over the years. According to Glassdoor, a customer service supervisor makes between $55,000 and $72,000 a year, while a customer service representative can expect between $14,000 and $21,000 a year as an hourly employee. Managers at Netflix can make between $72,000 and $304,000 per year. Software engineers make between $77,000 and $187,000 annually. A director of content's annual salary is between $192,000 and $362,000.[8]

want and stay away for however long they want, as long as they get their work done and don't take advantage of the system. This policy also applies to new parents. In the United States, most workers aren't guaranteed paid maternity or paternity leave through their jobs. In fact, only around 13 percent of people who work for private companies have access to paid time off when they have a child.[9] For some other companies, eligible workers can take up to 12 weeks of unpaid leave following the birth of a child. But tech companies are often different. Facebook offers birth and adoptive parents four months of paid leave, as well as $4,000 in "baby cash." Apple gives expectant mothers up to four weeks before a delivery and 14 weeks after. Expectant fathers and other non-birth parents can take six paid weeks off.[10] Mothers or fathers working at Netflix can take as many days, weeks, or months as they need to spend time with a new baby. As long as they sign a contract that they'll return to work at an agreed-upon date, they have the freedom to explore new parenthood without worrying about getting laid off.

For many workers, Netflix's attitude toward time off is a boon. But the policy has also proven to be somewhat controversial. When faced with the idea of paid "unlimited" vacation, studies have shown that many

COMPENSATION SATISFACTION VS. INTEREST IN CHANGING JOBS[11]

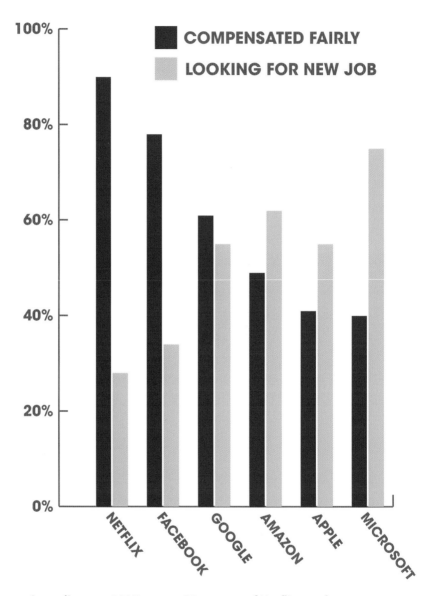

According to a 2017 survey, 90 percent of Netflix employees say the company pays them fairly. Less than 30 percent said they were looking for a job at another company.

employees end up taking less time off than they did before. Some are confused by the lack of clear guidelines on what's actually acceptable to managers. Others worry their coworkers won't approve of too much time away from collaborative or time-sensitive projects. Still, for Netflix employees, the option is there.

(TOO) HIGH STANDARDS

The aim of most top-rated companies is to staff a team that can transform the company's goals into real products and services. Treat employees fairly and reward them generously, and in turn they'll deliver the goods. But what happens when the drive for success overshadows all else? Can a company's enforced work ethic be so strict that it causes an excessive or unhealthy amount of stress?

In 2009, Netflix produced what it called the "Freedom & Responsibility" presentation. It was a collection of 125 PowerPoint slides that were created to recruit potential employees and communicate Netflix's corporate values to the existing staff and the world. For example, it listed the nine skills it valued most in its employees, including wise judgment; excellent communication skills, especially in stressful situations; a curiosity to learn in order to innovate new ideas; and the courage to take risks.

"We're a *team*, not a family. We're like a pro sports team, not a kids' recreational team. [The] coaches' job at every level of Netflix [is] to hire, develop and cut smartly, so we have stars in every position," one slide read.[12]

In 2017, Netflix's corporate executives updated the slideshow into a more concise text. The document discussed the importance of appreciating and fostering diversity in the workforce. It called out the need for intervention if a colleague was acting inappropriately or like a "brilliant jerk."[13] It also explained in plain and simple language what would happen if an employee wasn't measuring up to the company's standards:

> We focus on managers' judgment through the 'keeper test' for each of their people: if one of the members of the team was thinking of leaving for another firm, would the manager try hard to keep them from leaving? Those that do not pass the keeper test (i.e. their manager would not fight to keep them) are promptly and respectfully given a generous severance package.[14]

As the document makes clear, Netflix employees are allowed to have fun and play from time to time. But the reason they are hired is to work hard and deliver strong results. That can mean long hours and the near-constant threat of getting fired if they do not live up to Hastings's standards. This can be a debilitating influence on an underperforming employee's psyche. In fact, on the job search and anonymous employer review site Glassdoor, one of the most common complaints from Netflix employees addresses the "culture of fear" that exists around the office. As one particularly frazzled worker puts it, "[The] level of stress is high and I have been through so many team members being fired or let go that I can't even count them."[15]

For some Netflix employees, the drive to succeed brings with it a dangerous amount of pressure. Many employees worry about not doing enough

BOOTED FROM THE CULTURE SHE HELPED CREATE

Since the "Freedom & Responsibility" slideshow was created in 2009, it has been viewed more than 17 million times by Netflix employees and members of the public.[16] Other tech companies, such as HubSpot and Virgin Group, have adapted it to create their own mission statements. Facebook executive Sheryl Sandberg said the presentation "may well be the most important document to ever come out of Silicon Valley."[17]

Netflix's Patty McCord was responsible for creating the slideshow. She worked at Netflix for 14 years. During her tenure in human resources, she told hundreds of employees that their time at the company was over. But in 2012, she was forced out herself. She wasn't shocked. "When you agree that the number one priority is the right thing for the company and you agree that the person you report to gets to make the decision of what they want the team to look like, then you can't ever be surprised," she said.[18]

to please their bosses or not being able to keep up with the steady workflow. Others describe fierce competition with coworkers to stay relevant or toxic relationships with their managers. "When your management is stressed, it will always trickle down to create a lousy experience for you," one anonymous employee wrote on Glassdoor. "The high pay ensures that there is way more politicking than would be needed or appropriate in such situations. This in turn can have a very demoralizing effect on the [people] doing the actual work, who often feel compelled to work on nights, weekends, and public holidays for goals that are often vague and projects that are often shelved."[19]

In 2015, Netflix had approximately 3,700 employees. By 2017, that number had grown to 5,500 people.[20] For the most part, Netflix's staff is full of employees who work hard but mostly enjoy what they do. While many have been dissatisfied with the company after getting fired or quitting, others have left positive or balanced reviews on Glassdoor. They used words or phrases like "forward-thinking," "awesome," and "competitive." One particularly satisfied employee said, "This is the most interesting and engaging job I've ever had. Amazing benefits with great leadership and a feedback driven culture. Every day is a new challenge."[21]

Netflix has opened up offices around the world, including in Japan.

CHAPTER EIGHT

THE NETFLIX EFFECT

According to global information and measurement company Nielsen, Americans consumed nearly five hours of TV every day, on average, in 2013. That's about 34 hours a week and nearly 1,800 hours per year.[1] At that time, a majority of people still watched most of their content on a regular television, viewing live events or television series in real time or recorded on a digital video recording device.

But a lot has changed since then. Though Americans are still spending time in front of the television, the statistics are lower than in previous years, especially for the younger generations. For example, adolescents between ages 12 and 17 watched 11 hours and 47 minutes of traditional broadcast or cable TV per week in the second quarter of 2017. That's about

Netflix and other video-streaming services have significantly changed the media landscape in the United States.

45 percent less than during the same period five years prior. Older millennials, those between ages 25 and 34, watched 18 hours and 23 minutes per week in the second quarter of 2017, a drop of about 32 percent.[2]

These numbers suggest that people are either choosing to watch less television altogether or they are finding their content through other media. Some are swapping out part of their traditional TV-watching time in favor of streaming content on their phones, computers, or tablets. Others are cutting the cable cord altogether and going completely online. That's good news for digital streaming companies like Netflix.

"On one level, you're seeing things going from broadcast to cable and satellite networks, and now to internet networks. This ranges from things like YouTube, where you have pretty low-quality videos but interesting content, up to services like Netflix where you have very high-quality 4K video content," said Hastings. "People consume from multiple sources, just as they always have through the years. That's why we always focus on how our service can become better, because the competition is so strong."[3]

YouTube, a service on which anyone can upload their own content, has become the world's most popular way to watch streaming video.

NEW CONTENT, NEW VIEWERS

Binge-worthy content that's released all at once has become the norm in the 2010s. With the rise of the 24-hour news cycle—thanks to the advent of news-focused apps and the dissemination of current event headlines on Twitter and other social media outlets—more viewers are tuning in and enjoying escape-worthy content such as action thriller series.

Originally, company executives spent most of their time and money negotiating licensing deals for content created by outside studios. Now, in addition to buying a library of existing shows, Netflix is commissioning its own shows like it's a TV network. In the years since Netflix jumped into the content-making business with originally produced shows such as *House of Cards* and *Orange Is the New Black*, the company has transformed into a content production company to rival traditional studios.

The significance of this is twofold. In the past, broadcasters like NBC and ABC needed to make shows supported mainly by advertising revenue. This traditional model still exists today. But Netflix displays few ads, only beginning to show ads for its own programming in 2018. For the most part, it has to please only its subscribers. Therefore, the company can theoretically create movies and TV series for anyone with access.

In the traditional TV model, viewer demographics are typically broken down by categories such as age, gender, and race. Netflix collects more specific data based on what its customers actually watch, organizing people into groups it calls "taste clusters."[4] One cluster might like science fiction films. Another might like

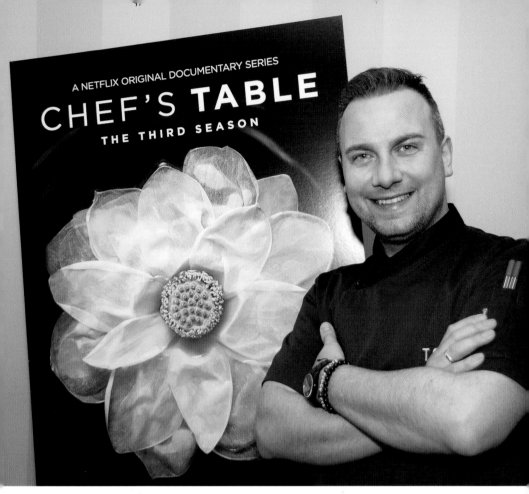

In addition to its dramas and comedies, Netflix rounds out its offerings with documentaries and a wide variety of other programs, including the nonfiction show *Chef's Table*.

romantic comedies. The company tracks nearly 2,000 of these clusters, giving it a clear sense of who its existing programs appeal to and helping it predict the kinds of audiences new shows might find.

With all this data in mind, Netflix launched 65 new original series, documentaries, and feature films in 2015, each of which appealed to a specific audience. *Master of None*, a show about dating and friendship in New York starring comic Aziz Ansari and writer Lena Waithe, was highly popular with millennials. Marvel's *Jessica Jones* wowed women and comic geeks alike by turning the superhero genre on its head and placing a savvy female private detective at its helm. *Chef's Table* built on traditional television's cooking shows to bring viewers inside the kitchens of some of the world's most famous culinary icons.

To keep up with HBO, Hulu, and the rest of its competition, Netflix added 600 more hours of original programming in 2016, with series such as sci-fi megahit *Stranger Things*; Baz Luhrmann's exhilarating song-and-dance phenomenon, *The Get Down*; and the popular period drama *The Crown*.[5] In 2017, it nabbed a record-setting 91 Emmy nominations for its shows.[6] The next year it earned 112 nominations, unseating HBO as the most-nominated company.[7] Netflix also promised to add more movies to the mix by producing at least 80 feature films in 2018.[8]

According to Sarandos, the movies would vary in subject matter, size, and cost. Some smaller budget films might clock in at $1 million, while a blockbuster gangster movie starring big-name actors Robert De Niro, Harvey Keitel, and Joe Pesci, and directed by Martin Scorsese, was projected to cost Netflix's production company $125 million. Of course, Netflix thinks the investment is worth it if it means attracting more viewers and pleasing already existing subscribers.

"Pretty dependably, a third of all the watching on Netflix is movies. In most places in the world, and from the beginning of our streaming initiative over 10 years ago," said Sarandos. "So I think people do look to us for movie entertainment."[9]

Looking ahead even further, the company is already searching for ways to reach new audiences. In 2018,

TED SARANDOS: CHIEF CONTENT OFFICER

Theodore A. Sarandos was born on July 30, 1964, in Phoenix, Arizona. His love for movies began in high school when he worked as a clerk at Arizona Video Cassettes West. Though he went on to study journalism at Arizona State University, Sarandos dropped out in 1983 to become store manager for the same video store chain. Eventually, his duties expanded and he managed a total of eight stores.

While serving as vice president of product and merchandising at the 500-store Video City/West Coast Video chain, Sarandos met Hastings. In 2000, Sarandos was hired as Netflix's chief content officer and public spokesperson for the company. He's also a member of Tribeca Film Festival and Los Angeles Film Festival boards. In 2013, he was chosen as one of *Time* magazine's 100 most influential people in the world.

In May 2018, Netflix announced a partnership with former president Barack Obama and former First Lady Michelle Obama to produce new programming.

Netflix announced plans to partner with mega-celebrity and Emmy-winning country music icon Dolly Parton on a series of eight made-for-TV movies about her life and career. Each film will be based on a classic Parton song, and the star will even appear in some of the films. "As a songwriter, I have always enjoyed telling stories through my music," Parton said in a statement. "I am thrilled to be bringing some of my favorite songs to life with Netflix. We hope our show will inspire and entertain families and folks of all generations."[10]

GLOBAL DOMINANCE

Netflix began as a small start-up in Scotts Valley, California. It shipped out DVDs to customers in a handful of regions in the United States. But in the 2010s, Netflix transformed into a truly global company.

In January 2016, the company expanded to 130 territories around the world, including countries such as Russia, India, and South Korea. This move tripled the company's distribution from the year before. "Today you are witnessing the birth of a new global internet TV network," said Hastings in a press conference. "With this

HIRING TRANSLATORS

In 2012, Netflix offered subtitles in three languages: English, Spanish, and Portuguese. When the company expanded to 130 countries in 2016, it upped its subtitle count to more than 20 languages, including Korean, Chinese, Arabic, and Polish. But many more languages were needed.

In 2017, Netflix issued a press release calling for all translators to apply for a job at Netflix. The company also created an online subtitling and translation test and invited people from all over the world to apply. Thousands did. "Our desire to delight members in 'their' language, while staying true to creative intent and being mindful of cultural nuances is important to ensure quality," a Netflix spokesperson said. "It's also fueling a need to rapidly add great talent who can help provide top-notch translations for our global members across all of these languages."[11]

Netflix is not only creating new programming but also making those shows available around the world.

launch, consumers around the world—from Singapore to St. Petersburg, from San Francisco to Sao Paulo—will be able to enjoy TV shows and movies simultaneously—no more waiting. With the help of the internet, we are putting power in consumers' hands to watch whenever, wherever, and on whatever device."[12]

Since then, Netflix has continued to hold its position. As of 2018, the company had more than 120 million members in more than 190 countries.[13] It was valued at more than $130 billion. Though in constant competition with digital content providers like Amazon and Hulu, Netflix was worth almost as much as industry giants Disney ($155 billion) and Comcast ($169 billion).[14]

Of course, there are still obstacles on the road ahead. The main one is staying ahead of competitors. Netflix has increased its subscription prices to account for its massive investment in new content. At the same time, HBO, Showtime, CBS, and other providers have added their own monthly subscription sites that vie with Netflix for people's money. Hulu is buying up rights to TV shows after some studios chose not to renew their contracts with Netflix as the company shifts its focus to original programming. In 2018, Disney began pulling all of its licensed content from Netflix. It also announced it would launch its own streaming service in 2019.

How long can Netflix remain at the top? That remains to be seen. But for his part, Hastings is not worried about facing off against his rivals: "I love competing, I love going up against Disney and HBO, that's what gets me going."[15]

TIMELINE

1997

Reed Hastings and Marc Randolph cofound NetFlix, an online company that sells and rents DVDs to consumers.

1998

NetFlix hires more staff; the company's website goes live in April; in December, NetFlix stops selling DVDs.

1999

NetFlix launches its first subscription service, which offers unlimited DVD rentals for a monthly price.

2000

NetFlix introduces CineMatch, a personalized movie recommendation system that uses members' ratings to predict future content-watching choices.

2001

The dot-com bubble bursts; NetFlix cuts 40 percent of its staff and moves from Scotts Valley to Los Gatos, California.

2003

Netflix reaches the milestone of one million subscribers; the company signs deals with more than 50 film distributors.

2005

The number of people with Netflix subscriptions reaches 4.2 million.

2006

Netflix announces a $1 million contest to create an upgraded version of the recommendation algorithm CineMatch; Amazon introduces video on demand.

2007

Netflix introduces its online streaming service; the service allows members to watch television shows and movies on their computers.

2008

Netflix makes deals with companies such as Microsoft and Roku to provide streaming on the Xbox 360 and TV set-top boxes.

2010

Netflix launches in Canada; its content is available on the Apple iPhone and other internet-connected devices; Blockbuster files for bankruptcy.

2011

Netflix becomes available throughout Latin America and the Caribbean; Hastings announces the launch of Qwikster, the short-lived spin-off company of Netflix.

2013

Netflix makes all episodes of its original show *House of Cards* available to the public at once, sparking the binge-watching phenomenon.

2017

By the end of the year, Netflix has 117 million subscribers; the company announces it will spend up to $8 billion on new content in the next year.

2018

Netflix has more than 120 million subscribers worldwide.

ESSENTIAL **FACTS**

KEY PLAYERS

FOUNDERS

- Reed Hastings, Marc Randolph

CEOs

- Reed Hastings (co-CEO from 1998–1999)
- Marc Randolph (co-CEO from 1998–1999)
- Reed Hastings (sole CEO from 1999)

KEY STATISTICS

- In 2017, Netflix subscribers collectively watched more than 140 million hours of TV shows and movies per day on average.
- As of 2018, Netflix has more than 120 million members in more than 190 countries.
- Netflix had approximately 5,500 full-time employees in 2017.
- Netflix's "Freedom & Responsibility" slideshow presentation has more than 17 million online views since it was created in 2009.
- Netflix's CEO Reed Hastings has a net worth of $4 billion.

IMPACT ON HISTORY

Prior to Netflix's launch in 1998, the film-rental world was controlled by three companies: Blockbuster, Hollywood Video, and Movie Gallery. People rented movies by going to a physical store and browsing the shelves. But Netflix upended that business model by first creating a DVD-by-mail company, then adding a subscription service that would allow its members to rent a certain number of movies per month, with no late fees. The company disrupted the industry again in 2007 by adding an online streaming service, which prompted a binge-watching craze in millions of American households. Perhaps the most impactful shift was Netflix's foray into producing original content. In 2018, it was nominated for a whopping 112 Emmy Awards, toppling industry rival HBO. Netflix is now one of the largest media companies in the world. Its trendsetting services are available in more than 190 countries worldwide.

QUOTE

"The dream 20 years from now is to have a global entertainment distribution company that provides a unique channel for film producers and studios. Starbucks is a great example. [Starbucks CEO] Howard Schultz talks about building the brand one cup at a time. I'd love to be Howard Schultz. As Starbucks is for coffee, Netflix is for movies."

—Reed Hastings, 2002

GLOSSARY

algorithm
A set of steps followed to solve a mathematical problem
or to complete a computer process.

austere
Strict or severe.

bandwidth
The rate at which computer data is sent from one point
to another.

brick-and-mortar
Having a physical building where customers go to shop
(as opposed to a website).

impromptu
Sudden and unplanned.

MP3
A type of compressed audio file that takes up a
small amount of space and can be easily shared or
downloaded by consumers.

prime time
   The period in the evening when the most popular shows are often scheduled on broadcast or cable television.

simultaneously
   Happening at the same time.

streaming
   Broadcasting live video over the internet.

tenure
   The amount of time spent in a job or office.

VHS
   An outdated type of videocassette tape that was able to record, play back, and store content, such as movies.

ADDITIONAL **RESOURCES**

SELECTED BIBLIOGRAPHY

Keating, Gina. *Netflixed*: *The Epic Battle for America's Eyeballs*. Portfolio/Penguin, 2012. Print.

Wu, Tim. "Netflix's War on Mass Culture." *The New Republic*, 4 Dec. 2013, newrepublic.com. Accessed 30 Apr. 2018.

Xavier, Jon. "Netflix's First CEO on Reed Hastings and How the Company Really Got Started." *Silicon Valley Business Journal*, 8 Jan. 2014, bizjournals.com. Accessed 30 Apr. 2018.

FURTHER READINGS

Lusted, Marcia Amidon. *Netflix: The Company and Its Founders*. Abdo, 2013.

Naber, Therese. *How the Computer Changed History*. Abdo, 2016.

ONLINE RESOURCES

Booklinks
NONFICTION NETWORK
FREE! ONLINE NONFICTION RESOURCES

To learn more about Netflix, visit **abdobooklinks.com**. These links are routinely monitored and updated to provide the most current information available.

MORE INFORMATION

For more information on this subject, contact or visit the following organizations:

COMPUTER HISTORY MUSEUM
1401 N. Shoreline Blvd.
Mountain View, CA 94043
650-810-1010
computerhistory.org
This museum presents a fascinating history of computers and their development. Rotating in-person and online exhibits explore topics such as self-driving cars, the history of the internet, the rise of Silicon Valley, and more.

THE TECH MUSEUM OF INNOVATION
201 South Market St.
San Jose, CA 95113
408-294-8324
thetech.org
Learn about Silicon Valley's history and the fascinating world of engineering design while visiting the Tech Museum. Visitors can browse exhibits about the latest and greatest innovations in tech.

SOURCE **NOTES**

CHAPTER 1. NETFLIX'S DEEP POCKETS

1. Dana Feldman. "The Most Binged Shows on Netflix in 2017." *Forbes*, 11 Dec. 2017, forbes.com. Accessed 12 Aug. 2018.

2. John Koblin. "Netflix Says It Will Spend Up to $8 Billion on Content Next Year." *New York Times*, 16 Oct. 2017, nytimes.com. Accessed 30 Apr. 2018.

3. Todd Spangler. "Netflix Blasts Past Q4 Subscriber-Growth Expectations, Shares Soar to All-Time High." *Variety*, 22 Jan. 2018, variety.com. Accessed 30 Apr. 2018.

4. "About Netflix." *Netflix*, n.d., netflix.com. Accessed 30 Apr. 2018.

5. Rani Molla. "Netflix Spends More on Content Than Anyone Else on the Internet—and Many TV Networks, Too." *Recode*, 26 Feb. 2018, recode.net. Accessed 12 Aug. 2018.

6. Elizabeth Gurdus. "Cramer Pinpoints the Key Strategy Driving Netflix's Success." *Mad Money*, 18 July 2017, cnbc.com. Accessed 30 Apr. 2018.

7. "Netflix Declares Binge Watching Is the New Normal." *Netflix*, 13 Dec. 2013, netflix.com. Accessed 30 Apr. 2018.

8. Ruth Spencer. "With Netflix Releasing House of Cards All at Once, Tell Us About Your TV Binges." *Guardian*, 5 Feb. 2013, theguardian.com. Accessed 12 Aug. 2018.

9. "Netflix Declares Binge Watching Is the New Normal."

10. "Netflix Declares Binge Watching Is the New Normal."

11. Rani Molla. "Netflix Now Has Nearly 118 Million Streaming Subscribers Globally." *Recode*, 22 Jan. 2018, recode.net. Accessed 22 Jan. 2018.

12. "CNBC Transcript: Netflix Founder and CEO Reed Hastings Speaks with CNBC's Julia Boorstin on 'Squawk Alley' Today from the Code Conference." *CNBC*, 31 May 2017, cnbc.com. Accessed 30 Apr. 2018.

13. Carrie Witmer. "The 11 Worst Netflix Original Shows of All Time, According to Critics." *Business Insider*, 1 Sept. 2017, businessinsider.com. Accessed 30 Apr. 2018.

CHAPTER 2. A EUREKA MOMENT

1. Gina Keating. *Netflixed: The Epic Battle for America's Eyeballs*. Penguin, 2012. 2.

2. Daniel Schorn. "The Brain behind Netflix." *60 Minutes*, 1 Dec. 2006, cbsnews.com. Accessed 30 Apr. 2018.

3. Michelle Castillo. "Reed Hastings' Story about the Founding of Netflix Has Changed Several Times." *CNBC*, 23 May 2017, cnbc.com. Accessed 30 Apr. 2018.

4. Jon Xavier. "Netflix's First CEO on Reed Hastings and How the Company Really Got Started." *Silicon Valley Business Journal*, 8 Jan. 2014, bizjournals.com. Accessed 30 Apr. 2018.

5. Britanny Hodak. "RIP VHS: World's Last VCR Will Be Made This Month." *Forbes*, 23 July 2016, forbes.com. Accessed 12 Aug. 2018.

6. "Netflix, Inc. History." *Funding Universe*, n.d., fundinguniverse.com. Accessed 30 Apr. 2018.

7. Xavier, "Netflix's First CEO on Reed Hastings."

8. Xavier, "Netflix's First CEO on Reed Hastings."

CHAPTER 3. FOUNDING NETFLIX

1. "Reed Hastings." *Famous Entrepreneurs*, n.d., famous-entrepreneurs.com. Accessed 12 Aug. 2018.

2. "Reed Hastings." *Forbes*, n.d., forbes.com. Accessed 30 Apr. 2018.

3. "Netflix Offers First of Its Kind National DVD Promotion Online." *Netflix*, 14 Apr. 1998, media.netflix.com. Accessed 12 Aug. 2018.

4. Jon Xavier. "Netflix's First CEO on Reed Hastings and How the Company Really Got Started." *Silicon Valley Business Journal*, 8 Jan. 2014, bizjournals.com. Accessed 30 Apr. 2018.

5. Gina Keating. *Netflixed: The Epic Battle for America's Eyeballs*. Penguin, 2012. 34.

CHAPTER 4. A ROCKY FIRST YEAR

1. Gina Keating. *Netflixed: The Epic Battle for America's Eyeballs*. Penguin, 2012. 44.

2. Keating, *Netflixed*, 34–35.

3. Keating, *Netflixed*, 34–35.

4. Keating, *Netflixed*, 34–35.

5. "Netflix, Inc. History." *Funding Universe*, n.d., fundinguniverse.com. Accessed 30 Apr. 2018.

6. Keating, *Netflixed*, 48.

7. Keating, *Netflixed*, 52.

8. Keating, *Netflixed*, 34–35.

9. Jon Xavier. "Netflix's First CEO on Reed Hastings and How the Company Really Got Started." *Silicon Valley Business Journal*, 8 Jan. 2014, bizjournals.com. Accessed 30 Apr. 2018.

10. "Netflix, Inc. History."

11. "Netflix, Inc. History."

12. "Offering of Netflix Brings in $82.5 Million." *New York Times*, 23 May 2002, nytimes.com. Accessed 12 Aug. 2018.

13. Keating, *Netflixed*, 59.

14. Keating, *Netflixed*, 63.

CHAPTER 5. NETFLIX RESTRUCTURES

1. "Netflix, Inc. History." *Funding Universe*, n.d., fundinguniverse.com. Accessed 30 Apr. 2018.

2. "Offering of Netflix Brings in $82.5 Million." *New York Times*, 23 May 2002, nytimes.com. Accessed 12 Aug. 2018.

3. Jon Xavier. "Netflix's First CEO on Reed Hastings and How the Company Really Got Started." *Silicon Valley Business Journal*, 8 Jan. 2014, bizjournals.com. Accessed 30 Apr. 2018.

4. Jeffrey M. O'Brien. "The Netflix Effect." *Wired*, 1 Dec. 2012, wired.com. Accessed 12 Aug. 2018.

5. Gina Keating. *Netflixed: The Epic Battle for America's Eyeballs*. Penguin, 2012. 86.

6. "Netflix, Inc. History."

7. O'Brien, "The Netflix Effect."

8. Keating, *Netflixed*, 98.

CHAPTER 6. FROM DVDS TO STREAMING

1. "Internet/Broadband Fact Sheet." *Pew Research Center*, 5 Feb. 2018, pewinternet.org. Accessed 12 Aug. 2018.

2. "Netflix Takes Movies on the Road with the '2006 Netflix Rolling Roadshow' Summer Screening Festival." *Netflix*, 2 May 2006, media.netflix.com. Accessed 12 Aug. 2018.

3. Gina Keating. *Netflixed: The Epic Battle for America's Eyeballs*. Penguin, 2012. 164.

4. Keating, *Netflixed*, 164.

5. Keating, *Netflixed*, 186.

6. Keating, *Netflixed*, 168.

7. Quentin Hardy. "Netflix to Stream Live Movies for Free." *Forbes*, 16 Jan. 2017, forbes.com. Accessed 30 Apr. 2018.

8. Keating, *Netflixed*, 225.

9. Keating, *Netflixed*, 227.

10. "Netflix Hints at Canadian Expansion Success." *CBC*, 24 Dec. 2010, cbc.ca. Accessed 12 Aug. 2018.

11. "Netflix Launches in Sweden, Denmark, Norway, and Finland." *PR Newswire*, 18 Oct. 2012, prnewswire.com. Accessed 30 Apr. 2018.

12. "Netflix Hints at Canadian Expansion Success."

13. Keating, *Netflixed*, 248.

14. Keating, *Netflixed*, 250.

15. Keating, *Netflixed*, 251.

16. Keating, *Netflixed*, 254.

CHAPTER 7. NETFLIX CULTURE

1. Kevin Roose. "Photos: Offices in Silicon Valley That Are Way Better Than Yours." *New York*, 5 June 2014, nymag.com. Accessed 30 Apr. 2018.

2. Debra Birnbaum and Gene Maddaus. "Netflix Moves to New Hollywood Office Next Week." *Variety*, 15 Feb. 2017, variety.com. Accessed 30 Apr. 2018.

3. Todd Spangler. "Netflix Leases Even More Space at Hollywood's Sunset Bronson Studios." *Variety*, 12 July 2017, variety.com. Accessed 30 Apr. 2018.

4. Janko Roettgers. "How Netflix Ticks: Five Key Insights from the Company's New Corporate Culture Manifesto." *Variety*, 21 June 2017, variety.com. Accessed 30 Apr. 2018.

5. "Netflix Salaries." *Comparably*, n.d., comparably.com. Accessed 30 Apr. 2018.

6. Gus Lubin. "Google Has the Highest Average Salaries in the Tech Industry: $141,000." *Business Insider*, 10 June 2011, businessinsider.com. Accessed 12 Aug. 2018.

7. "Usual Weekly Earnings of Wage and Salary Workers, Second Quarter 2018." *Bureau of Labor Statistics*, 17 July 2018, bls.gov. Accessed 12 Aug. 2018.

8. "Netflix Salaries." *Glassdoor*, n.d., glassdoor.com. Accessed 12 Aug. 2018.

9. Kathryn Vasel. "Calls for Paid Family Leave Are Getting Louder." *CNN Money*, 13 Feb. 2018, money.cnn.com. Accessed 12 Aug. 2018.

10. Rebecca Grant. "Silicon Valley's Best and Worst Jobs for New Moms (and Dads)." *Atlantic*, 2 Mar. 2015. Accessed 12 Aug. 2018.

11. Nate Swanner. "Netflix Shows Perks Matter as Much as Pay." *Dice*, 8 Nov. 2017, insights.dice.com. Accessed 12 Aug. 2018.

12. "We're a Team, Not a Family." *SlideShare*, 30 June 2011, slideshare.net. Accessed 12 Aug. 2018.

13. Roettgers, "How Netflix Ticks."

14. Roettgers, "How Netflix Ticks."

15. "Netflix Reviews." *Glassdoor*, n.d., glassdoor.com. Accessed 12 Aug. 2018.

16. Vivan Giang. "She Created Netflix's Culture and It Ultimately Got Her Fired." *Fast Company*, 17 Feb. 2016, fastcompany.com. Accessed 30 Apr. 2018.

17. Jay Rao. "What Silicon Valley Gets Wrong (and Right) about Culture." *Quartz*, 14 Apr. 2018, work.qz.com. Accessed 30 Apr. 2018.

18. Giang, "She Created Netflix's Culture."

19. "Netflix Reviews."

20. "Number of Netflix Employees from 2015 to 2017, by Type." *Statista*, 2018, statista.com. Accessed 12 Aug. 2018.

21. "Netflix Reviews."

CHAPTER 8. THE NETFLIX EFFECT

1. Tim Wu. "Netflix's War on Mass Culture." *New Republic*, 4 Dec. 2013, newrepublic.com. Accessed 30 Apr. 2018.

2. "The State of Traditional TV: Updated with Q2 2017 Data." *Marketing Charts*, 13 Dec. 2017, marketingcharts.com. Accessed 12 Aug. 2018.

3. "Netflix CEO Reed Hastings on the Future of Streaming, Competition and More." *Entrepreneur*, 21 Apr. 2016, entrepreneur.com. Accessed 12 Aug. 2018.

4. Josef Adalian. "Inside the Binge Factory." *Vulture*, 11 June 2018, vulture.com. Accessed 12 Aug. 2018.

5. Darrell Etherington. "Netflix Wants 50% of Its Library to Be Original Content." *TechCrunch*, 21 Sept. 2016, techcrunch.com. Accessed 30 Apr. 2018.

6. Josef Adalian. "How Netflix Broke HBO's 17-Year Emmys Streak." *Vulture*, 12 July 2018, vulture.com. Accessed 12 Aug. 2018.

7. Adalian, "How Netflix Broke HBO's 17-Year Emmys Streak."

8. Todd Spangler. "Netflix Plans to Release at Least 80 Original Films in 2018." *Variety*, 16 Oct. 2017, variety.com. Accessed 30 Aug. 2018.

9. Danny Vena. "4 Must-See Quotes from Netflix's Chief Content Officer." *Motley Fool*, 12 Dec. 2017, fool.com. Accessed 12 Aug. 2018.

10. Stephen L. Betts. "Dolly Parton to Produce Eight New Films for Netflix." *Rolling Stone*, 4 June 2018, rollingstone.com. Accessed 12 Aug. 2018.

11. "Netflix Is Looking for the Best Translators around the Globe." *Netflix*, 20 Mar. 2017, media.netflix.com. Accessed 12 Aug. 2018.

12. Ben Popper. "Netflix Announces It's Now Live in 130 New Countries Including India and Russia." *Verge*, 6 Jan. 2016, theverge.com. Accessed 30 Apr. 2018.

13. Alex Shephard. "Can Netflix Take Over Hollywood?" *New Republic*, 24 Apr. 2018, newrepublic.com. Accessed 30 Apr. 2018.

14. Todd Spangler. "Netflix Stock Pops to New All-Time High." *Variety*, 2 Mar. 2018, variety.com. Accessed 10 Sept. 2018.

15. Erin Griffith. "Netflix Sees Itself as the Anti-Apple." *Wired*, 15 Apr. 2018, wired.com. Accessed 30 Apr. 2018.

INDEX

ABOUT THE **AUTHOR**

ALEXIS BURLING

Alexis Burling has written dozens of articles and books for young readers on a variety of topics, including current events and biographies of famous people, nutrition and fitness, and careers and money management. She is also a professional book critic with reviews of adult and young adult books, author interviews, and other articles published in the *New York Times*, the *Washington Post*, the *San Francisco Chronicle*, and more. Burling lives in Portland, Oregon, with her husband.